The Gifted Kids Survival Guide

FOR AGES 10 & UNDER

Best wishes!

Judy Galbraith

The Gifted Kids Survival Guide

FOR AGES 10 & UNDER

Judy Galbraith

Free Spirit
PUBLISHING®

ISBN: 0-915793-00-8

Free Spirit Publishing Inc.
400 First Avenue North, Suite 616
Minneapolis, MN 55401

Library of Congress Catalog Card Number: 83-083015

Galbraith, Judy. 1954-
  The gifted kids survival guide
  1. Gifted Children. 2. Education. 3. Title
Printed in the United States of America

20 19 18 17 16

Original illustrations by Priscilla Kiedrowski

Also by Judy Galbraith: **THE GIFTED KIDS SURVIVAL GUIDE**
                          (For Ages 11-18)
                          Free Spirit Publishing
                          ISBN: 0-915793-01-6

To the people in my life who have encouraged me to take risks, work hard, stay playful and do more than I ever thought I could.

TABLE OF CONTENTS

★ When kids tease you for knowing so much or for getting perfect papers, do you ever wish you weren't so smart?

★ Do you ever wonder why you finish school work ahead of others in your class?

*Many gifted kids told us they didn't like the label gifted. Some preferred words like smart, intelligent or talented. Rather than use all of those words, we've decided to make things easier by shortening gifted and talented to GT. We'll use that abbreviation throughout the book.

★ When you think about things that no one else thinks of, do you wonder why your brain works the way it does?

★ Parents, teachers and even friends expect a lot of you. Do you sometimes wish they didn't?

★ Do you ever wonder what the heck labels like gifted, talented, high potential or high IQ *really* mean?

If you can say yes to any of these questions, then this book is especially for you.

It's been written with the help of hundreds of GTs like you who have some very important questions about what it means to be gifted and talented.

Most of the time, GT questions go unanswered. But not any more. **THE GIFTED KIDS SURVIVAL GUIDE** will answer your questions about why you think and learn the way you do, why school often isn't cool for GTs and what to do about it, and why GTs often have a tough time getting others to truly understand.

We know we won't be able to solve all of your problems or answer all of your questions. But we're sure we'll help you with the hassles that most often give GTs grief.

Together we'll learn about the six great gripes of gifted kids your age:

The Six Great Gripes of Gifted Kids

1. No one explains what being gifted is *all* about — it's kept a big secret.

2. The stuff we do in school is too easy and it's boring.

3. Kids often tease us about being smart.

4. Friends who really understand us are few and far between.

5. Parents, teachers (and even friends) expect us to be perfect, to "do our best" all the time.

6. We feel too different and wish people would accept us for what we are.

You can probably add a few of your own:

1. _____

2. _____

GTs tell us that by learning more about being gifted, they feel better about themselves and their abilities.

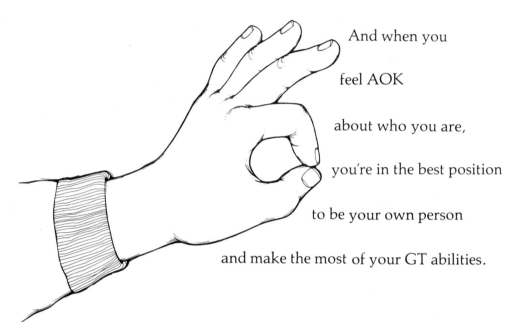

And when you

feel AOK

about who you are,

you're in the best position

to be your own person

and make the most of your GT abilities.

THE GIFTED KIDS SURVIVAL GUIDE has been written *for,* not just *about,* you. Feel free to: read it anyway you like, write in it, doodle down the sides of the pages . . . It's your book. And if there's anything we left out, please write and tell us about it. We'd love to hear from you.

Peace,
Judy Galbraith

Exposing The Secret

What Gifted and Talented Really Means

For most GTs, questions about giftedness start popping up when they're accepted into a program for the gifted and talented. Or teachers and parents may use euphemisms for GT if they feel uncomfortable with that label. So don't be fooled if your class is called the:

•High Potential

• Advanced Learner

• Exceptional Student
Search, Reach, Autonomous Learner, Challenge, or some other class name.

No matter what you call it, these groups are, for the most part, started for the same reason: To challenge students who need more stimulation than what the regular course work or the regular classroom teacher can provide.

GTs who are selected for such classes have a general feeling that it is a good thing. But according to many of the GTs we've talked to, no one bothers to tell you precisely what it's all about.

- Who else was chosen for the class?
- How did I get picked?
- Why isn't my friend in the class when he gets good grades too?

☞ **What the heck is going on here?**

Most of the time, you're left to figure it out for yourself because some people think giftedness should be kept a secret. It's almost as though gifted is a dirty word. In reality, it's usually because adults feel so uncomfortable with the word that information about giftedness isn't talked about in a straightforward manner.

Or parents and teachers may be afraid that the label will make you conceited, or that you'll feel too different from other kids.

But they're wrong. Dead wrong. When GTs find out about giftedness they **don't** get big heads and start feeling like a bunch of weirdos. Quite the contrary occurs.

When GTs find out about giftedness
They
Feel
Good!

Chances are, you've always known that you think and learn a little differently from many kids. Your friends may point it out to you when they say things like "you're so smart," or "you do everything right." But until now, no one has really put a finger on it and told you why you are the way you are. And as one girl commented, "No matter how much you try to look like everyone else, you'll always be different."

Being left to wonder about yourself is a very uncomfortable feeling.

The labels gifted, talented or high potential can help you to understand the differences and to feel good about them.

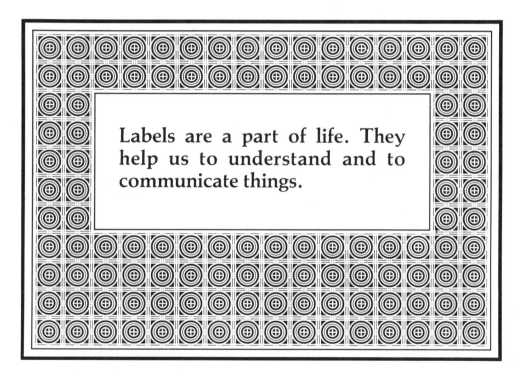

Labels are a part of life. They help us to understand and to communicate things.

Here are some things GTs wonder about when they think of the labels gifted and talented:

Questions about giftedness are difficult to answer and even the experts can't agree on a nice, simple definition.

So we're going to explain it a number of ways. First, we'll summarize some common definitions of gifted and talented. Then, we'll tell what GT means to the hundreds of kids we've talked to.

def′ə nish′ən

First of all, GT means different things to different people. And on top of that, there are many different *ways* of being GT.

But there is one thing most people do agree about when it comes to giftedness and that's POTENTIAL.

When you have high potential, it means your brain has the power to help you achieve great things *if you try.* You could be the smartest person in the world, but if you didn't try you'd be just as well off with a pea brain

"I never did anything worth doing by accident, nor did any of my inventions come by chance. They came by work."
—Thomas Edison

17

GTs who try, who use their potential, do things faster, with more intensity and accuracy than other kids their age.

Academic When gifted kids apply themselves in school, they may be gifted in one or more subjects: math, reading, social studies, spelling, science, music, art or phys. ed. As a result, many GTs are more challenged when they are ability grouped in school so they can learn new things rather than having to wait for others to catch up. Some GTs are put ahead a grade or two in certain subjects because they're ready for that level.

> *"I don't think size should determine what grade you're in at school. I think we should be grouped by how much we know. What does size have to do with anything?"*
>
> Scott, 9

What classes just seem to come naturally when you put your mind to work at them?

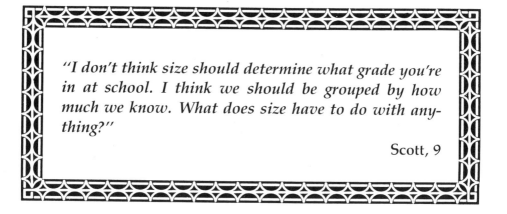

18

Another way of being gifted involves creativity. People who are highly creative are good at thinking up unusual ways to solve hard problems. (Have you ever come up with a way to do your math problems that's faster than the way your teacher taught you?)

Creative people may have unorthodox ways of doing things. They may be clever and able to think up their own jokes. Creative people like to be different.

Sometimes adults have a hard time accepting very creative kids because they often like to question why things are done the way they are done. Creatively gifted people like to break rules and this makes many adults feel uneasy.

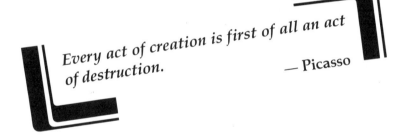

Every act of creation is first of all an act of destruction.

— Picasso

Talented performers are considered gifted in a special way. These people are best at expressing themselves through art, dance, drama or music. They're normally very creative and flexible. They like to show their stuff. Do you know anyone who fits this description? What's his or her special talent?

Leadership

If you're the kind of person who is organized and likes to tell people what to do, you may be a gifted leader. People with leadership ability are good decision makers, are popular and like to get people going. This is just one more area of gifted ability.

- Do you know someone who is a good leader?
- What makes them good in your opinion?

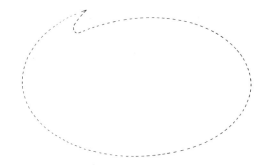

When you think about all of the different ways people can be gifted, it's mind-boggling. And we haven't even talked about all of those ways. It's easy to get frustrated trying to figure it all out. Just remember, there are no right or wrong answers here. Instead, there are many alternative ways of looking at, and defining giftedness.

Finally, here are some overall characteristics of GT ability that are good clues for identifying the gifted and talented.

While no person has all of these characteristics (not even Superman), most GTs show more than one of them.

GTs often:

Learn easily and quickly

Are persistent and want to keep trying

Ask a lot of questions and are very curious

Have good senses of humor

Dislike doing the same thing over and over and over and over and

Are very sensitive toward others

Think logically and want things to make sense

Are open to new, zany ideas!

Now that you know what adults think about giftedness, here's what GTs have to say about being gifted and talented.

Being ahead of the rest of the class

I don't understand it very well. I don't really know what it means.

To me, gifted means that I am above average, compared to most kids my age, in the ability to learn.

It means I am able to learn quickly or have deeper knowledge.

Intelligent, ambitious, interested.

Gifted means a kid who has potential and uses it.

It means high I.Q.

Gifted means
something special
to me... like
I've got
something good
going for myself.

Gifted means being
a little more smart
and creative than
other kids.

Gifted or high
potential means being
able to understand
grown-up jokes.

I think gifted means
people who have lots
of abilities and enjoy
many things.

It doesn't mean everybody
should treat me special.

Gifted means that
I'm talented in some
areas of school.

The most important question is:
What does gifted or talented mean to you?

Who Gets In Gifted Programs?

Most of the time, teachers or other school people choose GTs for special classes using several measurements such as:

- Achievement test scores
- IQ Scores
- Teacher recommendations
- Parent recommendations

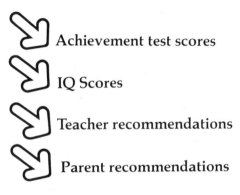

Achievement Test Scores

Achievement test scores tell how well you're learning things you are taught in school. The tests measure your progress in math, reading, science, social studies and other school subjects. You remember what those tests are all about: STOP! PUT YOUR PENCILS DOWN! DO NOT TURN TO THE NEXT PAGE UNTIL YOU ARE TOLD TO DO SO! Blah, Blah, Blah.

It's likely your scores will be a little different in each area because, as we said earlier, not all GTs are good at everything. But if you're chosen for a GT class, it's likely your scores are tops in more than one subject. In fact, many GTs' achievement test scores show them working at least two years beyond what kids their age normally do.

HI, IQ

IQ is the abbreviation for intelligence quotient. In simple terms, that is a score of how well you can accomplish school-type intellectual tasks. If your IQ is high, you have the potential to do very well in school. As we mentioned earlier, whether or not you *do* do well is entirely up to you.

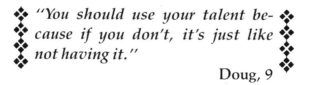

> *"You should use your talent because if you don't, it's just like not having it."*
>
> Doug, 9

What IQ scores *don't* show is how creative you are. Or what kind of athlete or musician or leader you could be. Or whether or not you have the motivation to use your GT brain. That's why it's important for adults to look at other things and not just IQ scores when they pick kids for gifted classes.

Teacher or Parent Recommendations

When parents or teachers recommend GTs for special classes, they usually write what they think and feel about your abilities. Sometimes the school gives them a checklist which tells them what to watch for in students. The checklist might look something like this:

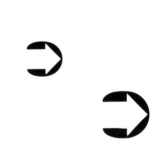

Teacher _Mrs. Magilicuddy_
Student _Pat. n._

Does the student:	Always	Sometimes	Never
1. Ask a lot of questions?	X		
2. Have lots of information on many things?	X		
3. Want to know how and why something is so?	X _(Pat's favorite word is "why.")_		
4. Seem interested in social problems?		X	
5. Stick to a subject or project long after the class has gone on to other tasks?		X	
6. Daydream?		X	
7. Understand easily?	X _(Pat learns concepts after the first explanation.)_		
8. Like solving puzzles and problems?		X	
9. Seem to be a loner?		X	
10. Love debating issues?	X		
11. Refuse to drill on math facts, spelling and handwriting?		X	
12. Criticize others for "dumb" ideas?		X	
13. Do things in unusual ways?	X		
14. Have a zany sense of humor?	X		
15. Invent and experiment?	X		
16. Have heightened senses?		X	
17. Pick up skills in art, dance or drama _(I don't know about these)_ without instruction?			X
18. Enjoy novelty and variety?	X		

Students who have many checks under the "Always" column are likely candidates for gifted education programs.

But even with checklists and test scores to help them decide who is GT, teachers and parents can make mistakes.

Here are some of the world's greatest contributors of the past, all misjudged at some time:

Believe It or Not!

- Beethoven's music teacher once told him that as composer, he was hopeless.

- Walt Disney was fired by a newspaper editor because he had "no good ideas."

- Winston Churchill failed sixth grade.

- Louisa May Alcott was told by an editor that she'd never write anything with popular appeal.

- As a boy, Thomas Edison was told by his teachers that he was too stupid to learn anything.

- Einstein was four before he could speak and seven before he could read.

How You Get To Be Gifted

We're sure we don't need to tell you that giftedness has nothing at all to do with gifts. No one is *given* high intelligence, creativity, athletic or leadership ability. But we do know that each of us has at least one pair of

That is, some of our giftedness is inherited which means one or both of your parents are GT too. Or maybe you inherited your giftedness from a grandparent or other close relative.

Our environment plays an important part, as well. From the day you're born, (and even while in the womb according to some*), everything about your lifestyle enhances or detracts from your abilities.

---

*In one study, mothers gave their unborn children reading lessons through a special audio transmitter. The transmitter was placed against the mother's stomach and it allowed the fetus to listen to reading tapes. Mothers would then read assignments through the transmitter as they did workbook lessons. Eighty-five lessons were given and the children received no other reading lessons until they started first grade. The results of the study showed that the children who received reading lessons *before* they were born had higher reading achievement test scores in elementary school than children who received no reading lessons until first grade. (Edward R. Sipay, "The Effect of Prenatal Instruction on Reading Achievement," Language Arts, January, 1983.)

That means, the more you:
    Read
    Travel
    Touch, feel, smell, hear and taste
    Meet new and interesting people, and
        Jazz up your life . . .
the more you turn ▊ your mind.

    Conversely, if you avoid:
    Trying new things
    Reading
    Meeting new people
    Doing anything except watching TV and
        shunning variety in your life . . .
You may as well turn your brain from ▊ to ▊ because
that is just about what it will do, TURN OFF.

    One place where you have an opportunity to keep your
brain turned ▊ is in school. Ironically, for many GTs,
school is a definite turnoff.

What's Uncool About School?

Ask any GT about school and he or she is quick to tell you that:

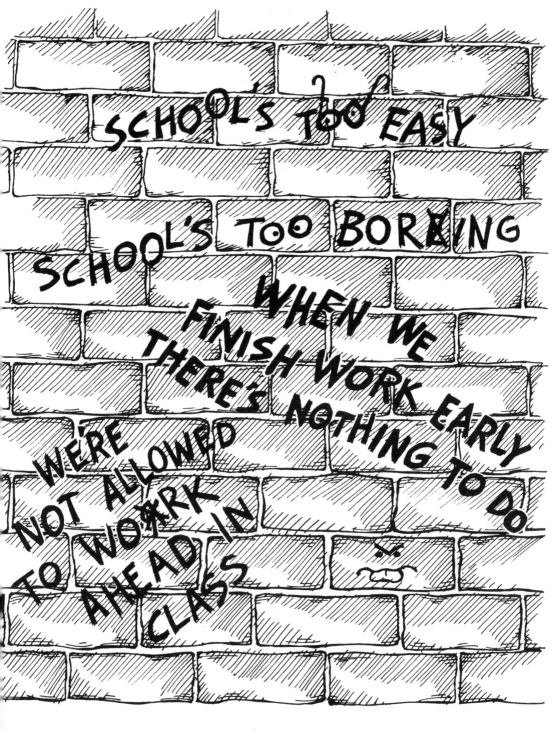

"Sometimes spelling gets so boring I just slop down any old thing on my paper."

Tara, 9

"When I can't work ahead in class I feel rejected by the teacher."

Heidi, 9

"I used to work ahead in class whenever I got done early . . . just to keep from getting bored. I quit doing that though, because when my teacher sees me working ahead, she just gives me worksheets or makes me clean the chalkboards."

Marty, 9

"When I finish assignments and there's nothing to do, I feel like I'm wasting my time in school."

Teri, 10

"I like to be able to get away from easy classes and have harder, more challenging ones."

Joe, 9½

"I feel MAD when I can't work ahead. Teachers should let you and be proud of you for it."

Tom, 8½

"It's just as hard for me to do hard stuff as it is for me to do easy work. Easy work just makes me tired."

Brad, 8

While you may not feel this way about school all of the time, we're sure you feel this way some of the time. And when you do, it's nice to know that *you don't have to accept things the way they are!*

The first and most important part about making school more challenging and interesting is to know just what you need to keep your brain turned ON. Nothing outrageous, just logical things like being able to:

➜ Learn at your own speed, not someone else's

➜ Pre-test out of work you already know and understand

➜ Study things of interest to you beyond basic schoolwork

➜ Work with ideas that really boggle your brain

The second thing you'll need to do to make school more right for you is to accept some of the responsibility for helping teachers learn how to teach you better.

"Somebody's boring me . . . I think it's me."
— **Dylan Thomas**

Remember that teachers have students of all different abilities to work with: slow learners, fast learners, kids with disabilities. They need your help in knowing how best to challenge you.

Ten Things To Do To Make
School More Cool

1. We've said it before and we'll say it again, talk with your teachers about **skipping over work you already know.** This will allow you time to do more challenging projects. For example, we talked to kids who take pretests at the beginning of their spelling units. If they score well on the pretest, they don't have to do the work for learning those words. (Why should they? They already know their stuff.) This same idea could apply to other subjects as well.

2. **Working independently** is a good way for you to study subjects in more depth than what usual classes allow. By working on your own thing, at your own speed, there's no limit to what you can learn. Ask your teacher to help you plan your study. Keep in mind that working independently doesn't necessarily mean working alone. GTs need help from others in learning the how-to's of independent study:

☞ These ideas suggest alternatives for GTs who want more out of school. While not all of these may appeal to you, we suggest giving some a try. We think you'll be more than happy with the results. And remember to be free to change your ideas to suit yourself: add on, elaborate, subtract from, elucidate, solicit suggestions from others.

What is it you'll study and how?

Who can help you? A librarian? Someone from the community?

How long will it take?

In what ways will you show what you've learned?

3. **What's your bag?** Is it art? Music? Dance? Drama? Find out if the special teachers in your school would be willing to accept your help in planning special events for fine arts activities.

4. **Be a display designer** and produce unique displays for your classroom or school. You could work on them alone or with others. Displays could be changed monthly and you would be in charge of putting them up and taking them down. Here are some more examples of displays produced by GTs we've talked to:

INVENTIONS AND INVENTORS

Enterprising and innovative GTs participated in an inventors fair and made a display to coincide with the event. They included information about famous inventors as well as their own inventions.

COLLECTIONS

Collections make great displays and most of the GTs we've talked with have at least one. (The most unusual collection we heard about consisted of hundreds of different sugar packets from restaurants all over the country.)

Included in one display were brief descriptions of each collection and information about how the collector got involved with that particular interest.

If you could start a collection that piqued your interest, what would it be? What would it look like?

5. If it's not on your school's menu, start your own recipe for **mini-classes.** For example, if you're interested in learning a foreign language, find a few others who share your interest. Talk with your teacher and the principal about your idea and have them help you figure out how, when and where you could have the class. They also may be able to help you find a tutor. Use language tapes from the library; add books and you're off. C'est une bonne idée!

6. **Doing double duty is a drag** and a common glitch of gifted programs. Often, GTs in special classes get stuck doing all of the regular class assignments *and* the work for their gifted class as well. For some GTs, this isn't a problem. But for many others the whole thing seems very unfair.

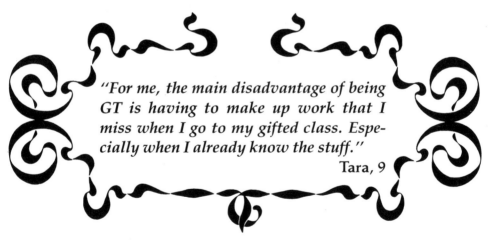

"For me, the main disadvantage of being GT is having to make up work that I miss when I go to my gifted class. Especially when I already know the stuff."
Tara, 9

GTs shouldn't have to do more work, or MOTS* work, just because they're gifted.

*MOTS = More Of The Same

GTs should be allowed to do different kinds of work. Don't be afraid to talk with your teacher about opting out of work you already know how to do so that you can work on some of the projects we're telling you about here.

7. **Volunteer** to help your teachers in creative and productive ways. (Cleaning chalkboards or being the class go-fer, for example, aren't creative activities in our book.) Can you help plan units? Media center directors and special teachers may welcome your help — could you be their computer aid, a tutor, or even a cable TV operator?

8. **Start a journal** for writing thoughts, poetry, stories, doodles, movie reviews, new ideas or other creative jottings in your spare time.

9. **Show what you learn in new and unusual ways.** Instead of writing the usual written report that's assigned, how about:
a diorama
an oral presentation
a slide show or photo essay
a mobile
a play
a song
a video tape

You fill in an alternative

If a man* does not keep pace with his companions
Perhaps it is because he hears a different drummer . . .
Let him step to the music which he hears
However measured or far away.

— **Henry David Thoreau**

10. Use your powers of persuasion and logic to convince your teacher that you need an "any time of the day" library pass. **Be a regular customer of the media center** and learn as much as you can on your own. While teachers try to do their best, they're not going to be able to teach you everything you want to know.

~ ~ ~

**The next best thing to knowing something
is knowing where to find it.**
— Samuel Johnson

*The words man and him are used in many verses but we're sure the authors meant to include girls and women as well.

What If My Teacher Says No?

Any time someone questions why things are done a certain way, he or she risks suffering resentment by a person who feels threatened by those questions or suggestions. As a GT, you need to recognize and accept that parents make mistakes, teachers make mistakes (and you make mistakes).

- Teachers don't always know what's best for you
- Teachers may say "no" to your suggestions, and
    They May Say Yes!

The grown-ups' response, this time, was to advise me to lay aside my drawings of boa constrictors, whether from the inside or the outside, and devote myself instead to geography, history, arithmetic and grammar. That is why, at the age of six, I gave up what might have been a magnificent career as a painter. Grown-ups never understand anything by themselves, and it is tiresome for children to be always and forever explaining things to them.

— Antoine de Saint Exupéry
THE LITTLE PRINCE

If you believe in yourself and your ideas, you need to be willing to take chances and keep trying even though things won't always happen in your favor.

You may have to restructure what you're asking for so your teacher will be more likely to say yes.

If your teacher says no, it may be a firm "No!" or it may mean, "Now is not the time to talk about this." But there is one thing we know for sure:

Unless you TRY, nothing cool will happen in school!

Last Resorts
Eight Things GTs Say They Do When They're Bored Silly In School

1. Draw, doodle

2. Finish homework so I don't have to take it home

3. Write stories

4. I fool around

5. Work ahead of the class (without letting the teacher know)

6. I twiddle my thumbs and am bored

7. I read a long, long book

8. Talk

Not Just For Girls Only

Girls, especially years ago, were often afraid to show their smarts. That's because people used to think that boys should be stronger, smarter and better than girls. They figured the boys would someday (when they became men) take care of the girls (women).

It's an old-fashioned idea and one that we can

KISS GOODBYE

Today, most people in our country and others as well agree: men, women, girls and boys can have equal rights and work side by side.

Sometimes girls try to hide the fact that they're smart or talented. They may worry that boys won't like them if they use their brains. A nine-year-old girl said,

"Boys don't like me because I'm smarter than they are."

But girls don't have to pretend they're dumb any longer. Men and women respect the work of:

★ **Sally Ride** — Astronaut and first U.S. woman in space
★ **Mary Decker** — Track Star; holds the world record in the 5,000-meter run
★ **Beverly Sills** — Opera Singer
★ **Sandra Day O'Conner** — U.S. Supreme Court Justice
★ **Barbara Jordan** — Former Congresswoman & Civil Rights Advocate
★ **Barbara McClintock** — Genetic Scientist, Nobel Prize for Medicine
★ **Gloria Steinem** — Author & Lecturer

These women are examples of girls who grew up and used their abilities to the max. Can you think of other women who kissed that old-fashioned idea goodbye?

If you could be famous for a great achievement, what would it be?

DAILY NEWS

50¢   Vol. 1   No. 1

New
Discovery!

GETTING ALONG GIFTED

According to GTs, one of the most bothersome things about being gifted is the teasing that comes with the label. And there are no two ways about it: when you're GT, you are going to be teased.

For some GTs, teasing isn't a big deal. They're able to go on doing their own thing and don't really care what other people say.

But many others feel differently:

"Teasing hurts, mentally and even physically at times."
Jeff, 9

Oftentimes, the teasing comes by way of not-so-fun nick-names:

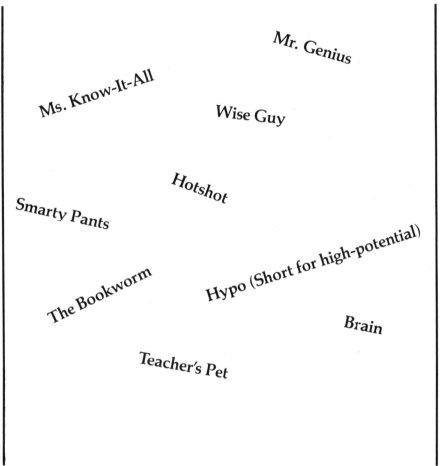

Mr. Genius

Ms. Know-It-All

Wise Guy

Hotshot

Smarty Pants

The Bookworm

Hypo (Short for high-potential)

Brain

Teacher's Pet

You've probably heard others and can add to our list:

Here's What GTs Have To Say About Teasing

People say you think you know a lot and you think you're big.

Angie, 9

I'm the editor of our school newspaper and if one mistake is made, everyone blames me.

Todd, 10

I get teased but I don't mind it because it's a good kind of teasing.

Pam, 9

Sometimes kids ignore you if you're too smart.

Andrea, 8

Sometimes kids are just jealous and that's why they tease.

Robert, 9

COPING WITH TEASING

In coping with GT teasing, it helps to know some of the reasons why kids tease:

— Kids may be jealous of you. They may wish they could do as well.

— Your friends may not know a better way of saying "I like you." (It's unfortunate, but people aren't very good at complimenting each other.)

— Classmates may feel inferior around you so they may put you down or criticize in order to make themselves feel better.

— They may not like you.

— Kids may tease just for fun. *All* kids get teased about something. If you weren't being teased about being GT, you'd probably be teased about something else.

Now that you know some of the reasons *why* kids tease, you can move to the next and most important part in coping with it.

Are you going to let teasing bug you?

The next time someone teases you about being smart or for doing something well, ask yourself three questions. Then see if you don't feel better about the situation.

? Who is doing the teasing? Is that person's opinion important to me?

? Why are they teasing me? Just for fun? Because they're jealous? Because they just plain don't like me?

? Do I accept the teasing? Am I going to let it get me down? Or am I going to simply ignore it and go on about my business?

If you automatically accept the teasing that comes your way, you're not in control of your feelings . . . someone else is. And if you worry too much about what other kids say, you may never be able to do what you really want to do. You'll be too busy trying to please everyone else.

GTs had this advice on how to cope with teasing:

"Just ignore kids who tease, or laugh along if they're your friends. It's just not important enough to get all worked up about."

If that doesn't work for you, here's another way to handle touchy situations:

1. Take a deep breath and count to three. Then, let the air out while counting to six. This will help you relax so you can talk without sounding MAD.

2. Stand straight and tall with both feet firmly on the ground.

3. Then, as you look the person in the eye, say politely how you felt when the person said the unkind thing. For example, "It makes me sad to hear that." or "It makes me angry when people make fun of others." (Try to remember to say how you *feel* so that you aren't insulting someone.)

4. You may ask for an apology, or simply walk away. The important thing to remember is that you have a right to express your feelings and to speak up for yourself.

5. Use your smarts, your words, your eyes, your whole body to stick up for rights.

Will The Real You Please Stand Up?

Submit to
pressure
from peers
and you move
down to their
level.
Speak up
for your own
beliefs
and you invite
them up to your
level.
If you move
with the crowd,
you'll get
no further than
the crowd.
When 40 million
people believe in
a dumb idea,
it's still a
dumb idea.
Simply swimming
with the tide
leaves you
nowhere.
So if you
believe in
something
that's good,
honest and bright—
stand up for it.
Maybe your peers
will get smart
and drift
your way.

Reprinted with permission from UNITED TECHNOLOGIES, Hartford, CT 06101

Ten Tips For
Making and Keeping
FRIENDS

We all need friends who understand and will share things with us. While it's important to have all different kinds of friends, GTs like and need to be with other kids who think and learn the way they do at least some of the time.

Here are some words of advice from GTs like you who, at times, find making friends a tricky proposition.

1. Don't act like a hotshot. That's wrong and it won't get you any friends.

2. Help kids to know that you have other interests besides schoolwork. Let them know you're more than just a super speller or a math whiz. Some of their interests may be ones you share too.

3. Get into a GT class if you can.

4. Be respectful and think about how other kids feel when you do things so well. Give them compliments when they do things well.

5. Don't always think you have to have things your way.

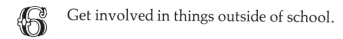 Get involved in things outside of school.

7 Be patient and try not to get aggravated when you're teaching someone something and he or she doesn't get it right away.

8 Don't feel weird about having friends who are older or younger than you are.

9 Be a friend.

10 When kids ask you for help, don't feel bad about saying "no." Sometimes you just don't have time. Sometimes you just don't feel like doing it. A true friend will understand.

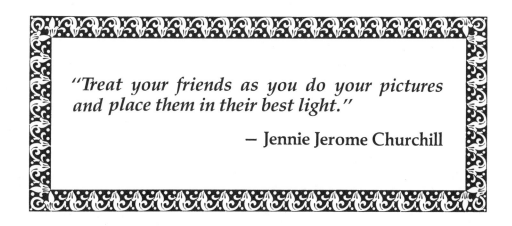

"Treat your friends as you do your pictures and place them in their best light."

— Jennie Jerome Churchill

If you were to give a piece of advice to GTs, what would it be?

_____

_____ ,

_____

_____

_____

_____

_____

_____

_____

_____

_____

_____

Do you follow the advice yourself?

54

GROWING UP GT

Just as being GT in school isn't always easy, being part of a gifted family is no cinch either.

Some of the hassles you have at home are probably not much different than what other kids have. Things like:

◆ Whose turn it is to do the dishes and take out the garbage,

◆ Not being able to consume unlimited quantities of junk food, or

◆ Deciding who gets to watch his or her favorite TV program.

The list could go on and on.

But GTs told us of a few hassles at home that other kids don't have to deal with.

GT Grief At Home
(And What To Do About It)

A. Parents have high expectations of us . . . they want us to be purrrrrrrrfect!

◆ *"Sometimes my parents just expect too much of me. They want me to get A's in every subject."*

Andy, 9

Andy said that he tried hard to do well in school and that he enjoys the challenge of working for A's. But he feels far too much pressure when his parents tell him they want A's all of the time.

Leslie's parents are more relaxed about her achievements. She had this to say,

◆ *"My parents are satisfied if they know I worked hard on something, even if I didn't get an A."*

Another boy had a different kind of complaint. His parents expect perfect behavior as well as good grades.

◆ *"My mom and dad expect me to be totally responsible for things around the house and not to play. They think it's a waste of time. I don't think that's fair."*

What To Do When Parents Pressure You

First, try to understand why parents want you to do so well at everything.

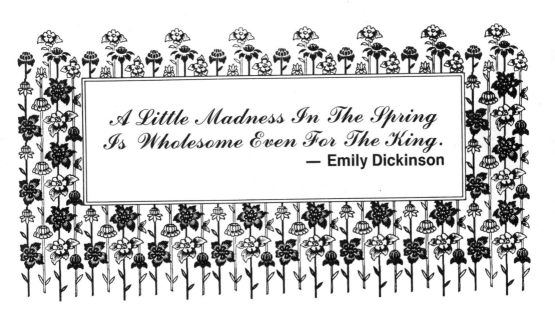

Parents want their kids to do well because it makes them feel that they are smart too, and they're doing a good job being parents.

Parents hear a lot about GTs needing to "work up to their potential." They may think that if you aren't getting A's, you aren't learning as much as you could be.

GT's sometimes act more grown-up than other kids their age and may be pretty responsible around home. When parents get used to your grown-up ways, they may come to expect that behavior *all* the time. So if you act kooky, silly, or just want to have some fun, they may think you're being irresponsible. (Now isn't that idea silly?)

A Little Madness In The Spring
Is Wholesome Even For The King.
— Emily Dickinson

Now that you know some of the reasons why parents have high expectations of you, you can begin to do something about it. First, you need to:

1 Talk with your parents about their high expectations. Let them know how you feel. Angry? Uptight? Unhappy? Inadequate? Like you'll never be good enough for them?

Once your parents know how their expectations make you feel, they'll be more likely to relax and try to accept you for what you are. If your parents aren't as understanding as you'd like, be sure to find some other supportive adult: another relative, a teacher, a neighbor.

2 Take it easy on yourself. GTs are often their own worst critics. They get in the habit of expecting so much of themselves that they become Nervous Nellies without any help from anyone else at all. Remember:

It's OK to: 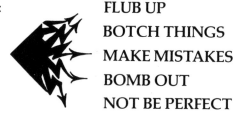 **FLUB UP**

BOTCH THINGS

MAKE MISTAKES

BOMB OUT

NOT BE PERFECT

(More on this later)

3 Remind parents, in a nice way, that they don't always do their best and yet, things usually turn out OK. Try to think of a time when you didn't do your best and still learned a lot or had fun. Ask your mom or dad to do the same.

B. Another hassle at home common to GTs has to do with relationships with

Oh Brothers, Oh Sisters!

"My brother is always trying to prove he's better than me and teases me about being a brain because I'm in the gifted class and he's not."

Sara, 9

All brothers and sisters argue about things. It's natural and it happens in every family. But GTs run into double trouble when school work is very easy for them and very hard for a brother or sister.

Siblings may be even more unhappy if you're chosen for the GT class in school and they aren't.

Here are some tips for getting along with brothers or sisters:

 Keep in mind that each person in your family is special in some way. All of you won't be good at the same things. Be sure to let your brothers and sisters know what you like and appreciate about them. Recognize their talents and tell them when they do something well.

59

If brothers or sisters tease you about being "a brain" or being in the GT class, remember it's likely they do it because they wish they could be in the class, too. Think about how you would feel if they'd been selected for the class and you hadn't. A little empathy goes a long way.

 Be patient. Try to understand that people learn in different ways and at different times. Your brothers or sisters may need more help and time to do things than you. They're not perfect. You're not perfect.

The Perfection Infection
(And Cure)

*The principal mark of genius is not perfection but original-
ity, the opening of new frontiers.*

— Arthur Koestler

GTs are, by nature, very susceptible to the perfection infection. When they get it, they find it nearly impossible to accept
anything done imperfectly. Perfect papers are in. Imperfect
papers are out. Drawings must be without flaw or it's the
wastebasket for them. And it's a very frustrating way to live
because **it is impossible to be perfect.** So if you've got the
perfection infection, and you think everything you do must
be just right, read on.

It's not hard to understand how GTs get the perfection bug
in them. After all, parents, teachers and even friends often
expect you to be flawless and faultless.

Colleen, 9, had a good example of how she's pressured to be perfect:

"When we have tests, people make bets to see if I'll get everything right. Then, if I don't get a perfect paper they say, 'If you're so smart, how come you got some wrong?' "

John added:

"A lot of people think that just because I'm good at some things I should be good at everything."

The Big Rip-Off

The rip-off for GTs who start believing this falderal is that they may:

Begin to feel inferior, or that nothing is ever good enough

Start doing things simply to please others rather than because it's what they want to do, or

Stop trying new things for fear of not being able to do them perfectly.

How To Cure The Perfection Infection

When you start feeling that nothing you do is ever quite good enough, either by your standards or someone else's . . . or you stop trying new things for fear of flubbing up, we hope you'll think about these truths:

I. Nobody is perfect and no one is good at everything.

Albert Einstein was one of the world's greatest scientists, yet he didn't learn to read until he was seven and he was terrible in math. Learn to give the things that are *most* important to you your maximum amount of energy. Then, give yourself a break and don't expect to go all out in everything else as well.

II. It's perfectly OK to be perfectly imperfect!

We know you've heard this adage before but we think it's worth repeating: We learn best by our mistakes. People who don't take chances and don't flub up aren't learning as much as those who do. (People who don't take chances don't have much fun either.)

III. Doing things perfectly doesn't make you a more successful person. Other things count too.

Getting an A in math or reading doesn't mean you're a nicer person, only smarter in math or reading. It's healthy to spend energies learning to care about and to help others.

We've talked a lot in this book about making changes and taking charge of your life. And that's great . . . as long as you have the guts to make the changes. This part of the book is all about how you can keep yourself from getting weak in the knees when you go to negotiate with your parents or teachers: How to be assertive so you get what you need.

Sticking Up For Your Rights

In sticking up for your rights, it helps to know just exactly what your rights are. Remember The Six Great Gripes of Gifted Kids? Well, you have the right to live WITHOUT the Six Great Gripes.

Six Great Rights

I. You have a right to be in classes that are challenging and interesting (not just MOTS*).

II. You have a right to know about giftedness and why you're in or should be in, a class for the gifted.

III. You have a right to make mistakes and "not do your best" if you feel like it.

IV. You have a right to be with other kids who really understand you.

V. You have a right to be treated with respect by friends, teachers and parents.

VI. You have a right to be different.

*More Of The Same

While none of these rights sound very outrageous, many GTs are not given their rights. So it is up to you to see that you get them.

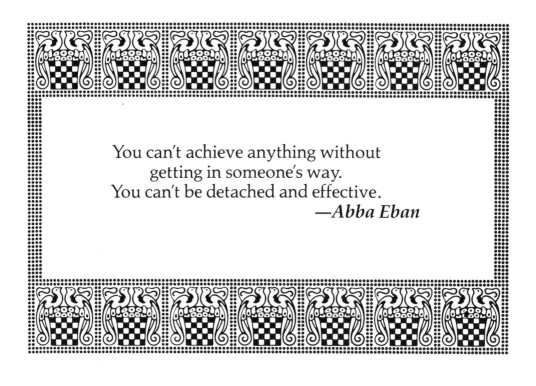

You can't achieve anything without
getting in someone's way.
You can't be detached and effective.
—*Abba Eban*

When you go to your teachers to ask for changes in school, or when you talk with your parents about things that concern you, here are a few do's and don'ts to help you along.

DO
1. Know what you want changed *before* your meeting and try to have as many facts to back up your request as possible.
2. Try to think about that person's position, how he or she feels, so you can anticipate any possible objections.

3. Pick a good time and place for your meeting. (Obviously if there's chaos in the room around you, getting special consideration may be very difficult.)
4. Start with a small request so you're more likely to succeed. Then, work up to bigger things once you've shown you can handle responsibility.

DON'T

1. Wait. Get started learning how to be assertive right now.
2. Blame people. It doesn't help.
3. Be uncompromising. If you give some, others are more likely to give too.
4. Stop trying. If at first you don't succeed, try something else.

Patience is a necessary ingredient of genius.
—Benjamin Disraeli

It isn't always easy being GT. But we hope we've made it a little easier by helping you understand more about yourself and giftedness. Most importantly, it's nice to know you're not alone.

We hope, with the help of this book, you will be free to be all you can be, and have fun along the way.

APPENDIX
Mind Expanding Magazines

Check to see if your school or local library subscribes to any of these magazines. If they do, you can preview them before sending in a subscription order. If they don't carry any of these magazines, talk with the librarian to see if he or she would be willing to order one or two of them.

Creative Kids — A Magazine By and For Creative Children. Jam-packed with art, stories, cartoons, interviews, photographs, games and more.
   Prufrock Press, P.O. Box 8813, Waco, TX 76714-8813

Cricket Magazine — Includes stories, jokes, contests, art and poetry.
   Carus Publishing, Box 300, 315 - 5th St., Peru, IL 61354

3•2•1 Contact — A science magazine published by The Children's Television Workshop. Full of Factoids, photography, questions and answers, puzzles and stories.
   Children's Television Workshop, 1 Lincoln Plaza, New York, NY 10023

Cobblestone — The history magazine for young history buffs.
   Cobblestone Publishing, 7 School Street, Peterborough, NH 03458

Zillions Magazine — Published by the Consumer's Union, this magazine provides advice and information on how to use money wisely.
   P.O. Box 54861, Boulder, CO 80322

National Geographic World — Produced for kids, this colorful magazine covers all that covers the world.
   1145 - 17th St. N.W., Washington, D.C. 20036

Recommended Reading

The Kids' Whole Future Catalog by Paula Taylor

The Anti-Coloring Book Series by Susan Striker

The Great Brain Series by John D. Fitzgerald

If You Want To Know More About Giftedness

In this book, we've mainly given you an introduction to giftedness. If you or your parents want to know more, call or write the organizations listed below and they'll do their best to answer your questions.

NAGC, The National Association for Gifted Children
1707 L St. N.W., Suite 550, Washington, D.C. 20036

CEC, The Council for Exceptional Children
1920 Association Drive, Reston, VA 22091

More Free Spirit Books

The Survival Guide for Parents of Gifted Kids: How to Understand, Live With, and Stick Up for Your Gifted Child
by Sally Yahnke Walker

Up-to-date, authoritative information about giftedness, gifted education, problems, personality traits, and more, written by an educator of gifted kids and their parents. For parents of children ages 5 & up.

$10.95; 152 pp.; illus.; S/C; 6" x 9"; ISBN 0-915793-28-8

The Ultimate Kids' Club Book: How to Organize, Find Members, Run Meetings, Raise Money, Handle Problems, and Much More!
by Melissa Maupin

Everything kids want and need to know to start and run a successful club of any type or size; for any reason, anywhere — at home, at school, in a community center, or place of worship. Ages 10-14.

$11.95; 120 pp.; S/C; 6" x 9"; ISBN 1-57542-007-4

Psychology for Kids: 40 Fun Tests That Help You Learn About Yourself
by Jonni Kincher

A creative, hands-on workbook to promote self-discovery, self-awareness, and self-esteem. Written by an educator, based on sound psychological concepts, and classroom-tested. Ages 10 and up.

$14.95; 152 pp.; illus.; S/C; 8 1/2" x 11"; ISBN 0-915793-85-7

To place an order or to request a free catalog
of SELF-HELP FOR KIDS® materials, write or call:

Free Spirit Publishing Inc.
400 First Avenue North, Suite 616
Minneapolis, MN 55401-1730
toll-free (800) 735-7323, local (612) 338-2068